EARTH
IN 30 SECONDS

This library edition published in 2016 by The Ivy Press Limited,
an imprint of The Quarto Group
6 Orchard Road, Suite 100
Lake Forest, CA 92630, U.S.A.
Tel: +1 949 380 7510
Fax: +1 949 380 7575

Distributed in the United States and Canada by
Lerner Publisher Services
241 First Avenue North
Minneapolis, MN 55401, U.S.A.
www.lernerbooks.com

First Library Edition

A CIP record for this book is available from the Library of Congress.

ISBN: 978-1-78240-385-2

Printed in China

10 9 8 7 6 5 4 3 2 1

EARTH
IN 30 SECONDS

ANITA GANERI

CONSULTANT: DR. CHERITH MOSES

Contents

Amazing Earth
... in 60 seconds

Planet Earth is amazing. It's just a tiny speck in the vastness of the universe, but it is the only planet we know of that supports life. Its age is mind-boggling—about 5 billion years old. Yet, new land can still form when volcanoes erupt. It is so huge that it would take you about 24 years to dig a hole to the other side. It is home to millions of different life-forms, some of them so tiny that you need a microscope to see them.

This book looks at fascinating topics about Earth, from our place in space to the importance of protecting our planet for the future.

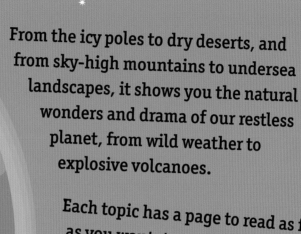

From the icy poles to dry deserts, and from sky-high mountains to undersea landscapes, it shows you the natural wonders and drama of our restless planet, from wild weather to explosive volcanoes.

Each topic has a page to read as fast as you want, to grasp the main facts quickly. There's also a speedy sum-up, to give you the basics in a nutshell. Then you can turn Earth detective and try the missions you'll find throughout. They will give you the chance to discover more about how your planet works. See for yourself why we have day and night, find out how mountains form, create a mini tornado in a bottle, and more.

Earth in Space

The universe is made up of millions and millions of galaxies, each traveling through space at incredible speed. Each one is made up of millions of stars. In our galaxy, named the Milky Way, eight planets travel around a star called the sun. The third planet from the sun is Earth. In this chapter, you can read about Earth's place in space and how the way that it moves causes day and night, and the seasons.

Earth in space
Glossary

axis An imaginary line through the center of Earth, around which it turns.

equator An imaginary line around Earth at an equal distance from the North and South poles.

galaxy Any of the large systems of stars, planets, and other objects in space—our galaxy is the Milky Way.

Milky Way The name of our galaxy, a large system of stars, planets, and other objects in space.

northern hemisphere The half of Earth north of the equator.

orbit A curved path followed by a planet or an object as it moves around another object in space, such as a planet, star, or moon.

planet A large ball-shaped object in space that moves around a star (such as the sun) and receives light from it.

poles The two points at the opposite ends of Earth's axis, known as the North Pole and the South Pole.

solar system The sun and all the planets that move around it.

southern hemisphere The half of Earth south of the equator.

universe The whole of space and everything in it, including Earth, the planets, and the stars.

Place in Space
... in 30 seconds

Planet Earth is one of eight planets that orbit the sun in space. Together with Mercury, Venus, Mars, Jupiter, Saturn, Uranus, and Neptune, the sun and Earth make up our solar system. Our solar system is a minute part of the vast universe, which is made up of everything that exists. It's hard to imagine!

Earth and the other planets travel around the sun in oval-shape paths, called orbits. Earth lies an average of 92,955,807 miles (149,597,871 km) away from the sun. It takes Earth about 365 days to orbit the sun.

Scientists believe that the whole of the solar system was formed from part of a vast cloud of gas and dust nearly 5 billion years ago. As far as we know, Earth is the only place in the universe that can support life. But who knows?

3-second sum-up

Earth is one of eight planets that orbit the sun.

3-minute mission Size Up the Solar System

You need: • Paper sheet 40 x 40 inches (1 x 1 m) • 22 inches (55 cm) of string • Pencil • Adhesive tape • Scissors • Ruler • Different-size sticker circles, and coins, counters, or lids • Extra paper

1 To draw the sun, tie the string to a pencil, leaving 20 inches (50 cm) loose. Tape the string end to the center of the large paper sheet. Pull the string taut to draw the circle.
3 Roughly match your stickers and circular objects to the planet diameters. Draw around them to complete your paper solar system.

DIAMETERS:
Sun: 39 inches
Mercury: 1/8 inch
Venus: 3/8 inch
Earth: 3/8 inch
Mars: 1/4 inch
Jupiter: 4 inches
Saturn: 3 1/4 inches
Uranus: 1 1/4 inches
Neptune: 1 3/8 inches

Earth is one of eight planets in the solar system. It is the third planet from the sun.

Neptune

Uranus

From space, Earth looks blue because two-thirds of its surface is covered in water.

Earth's year is 365 days long—the time it takes it to orbit the sun.

Earth's orbit

The length of Earth's orbit is 584 million miles (939.9 million km).

Mercury

Venus

Saturn

Sun

Moon

Earth

Mars

Jupiter

The sun is huge compared to Earth—109 Earths side by side would match the sun's diameter.

Spinning Earth

... in 30 seconds

We're on the move! Earth is spinning beneath our feet very slowly on its axis, an imaginary line running through the middle from the North Pole to the South Pole.

Earth spins all the time, but you do not feel any movement because it turns smoothly and at a steady speed.

It takes 23 hours, 56 minutes, and 4 seconds for Earth to spin around once on its axis. During that time, every place turns toward the sun and has daytime. Then it turns away from the sun and has nighttime. When it is daytime on one side of Earth, it is nighttime on the other. When you are getting up for breakfast, people on the other side of the world are getting ready for bed!

During the day, it looks as if the sun moves across the sky. In fact, it does not move at all. It is Earth that is moving. Earth always spins in the same direction, toward the east. So you see the sun rising in the east and setting in the west every day.

3-second sum-up

Earth spins on its axis, giving us day and night.

3-minute mission Spinning Earth

To see how we get day and night, find a basketball to be Earth and a flashlight for the sun. Tape outlines of the continents on the ball. Close the curtains. Turn the ball and ask a friend to shine the flashlight on it. You will see the outlines on the ball move into the light, then into the darkness.

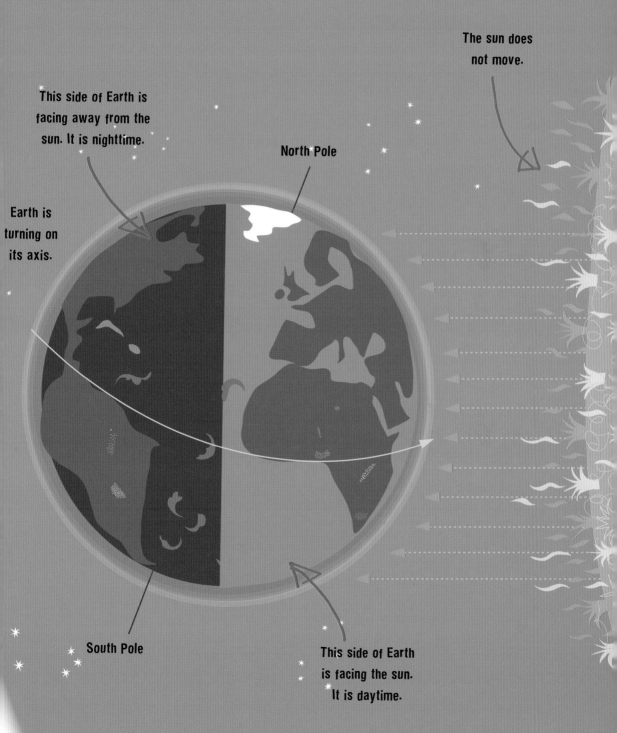

Earth spins around on its axis, but the sun remains still.

The sun does not move.

This side of Earth is facing away from the sun. It is nighttime.

North Pole

Earth is turning on its axis.

South Pole

This side of Earth is facing the sun. It is daytime.

Changing Seasons

... in 30 seconds

Did you know that Earth leans to one side? Earth is tilted on its axis at an angle of 23.5 degrees. As it orbits the sun, different places receive different amounts of light and heat throughout the year. This causes the seasons.

When the North Pole tilts toward the sun, it is summer in the northern hemisphere. The weather is warm and the days are long. Meanwhile, it is winter in the southern hemisphere. The weather is cold and the days are short.

When the South Pole tilts toward the sun, the seasons are the other way around. It is winter in the northern hemisphere and summer in the southern hemisphere. In between summer and winter, places that lie between the equator and the poles have spring and autumn. Each season lasts for about three months.

Places at the equator are not affected by Earth's tilt. They always lean toward the sun and are hot all year round. The year is divided into wet and dry times. At the poles, there are two seasons: six months of winter and six months of summer.

3-second sum-up

Seasons happen because Earth is tilted on its axis.

3-minute mission Show the Seasons

Hold up a globe—or a ball marked with the North and South poles. Ask a friend to hold a beach ball to be the sun. Tilt your globe and walk slowly around the sun. Stop when you think it is summer in the northern hemisphere. Are you right? Look at the illustration on the opposite page to check.

The seasons happen because different parts of Earth face toward and away from the sun during its orbit.

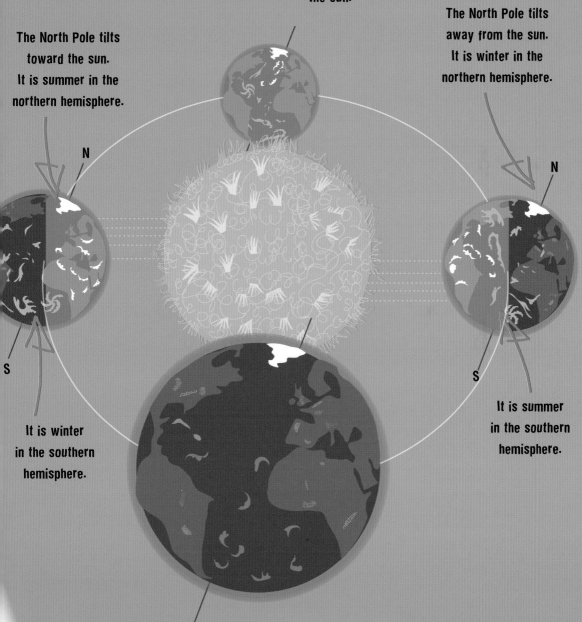

Earth is tilted on its axis as it orbits the sun.

The North Pole tilts toward the sun. It is summer in the northern hemisphere.

The North Pole tilts away from the sun. It is winter in the northern hemisphere.

N

N

S

S

It is winter in the southern hemisphere.

It is summer in the southern hemisphere.

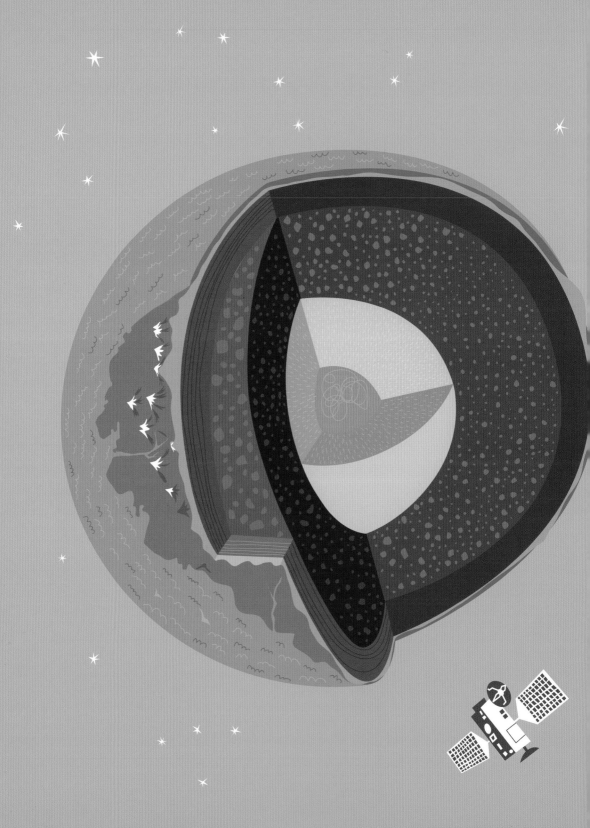

Earth's Structure

When you go for a walk, do you ever stop to think about what is going on beneath your feet? What is our planet actually made from? The ground you walk on is hard rock, but it doesn't always stay firmly in one place. Over millions of years, it has cracked and shifted, creating the continents and mountains we have today and causing dramatic earthquakes and volcanoes. In this chapter, you can read more about restless Earth.

Earth's Structure
Glossary

block mountain A mountain formed when cracks in Earth's crust force enormous blocks of rock upward.

continent One of the large land masses of Earth, such as Europe, Asia, or Africa.

continental drift The slow movement of the continents toward and away from each other.

core The innermost part of Earth.

crust The outer layer of Earth—the ground we walk on.

dome mountain A mountain formed when magma under the ground pushes the rocks above into a round bulge.

erode To gradually destroy and remove the surface of something through the action of wind, rain, or other natural elements.

fold mountain A mountain formed when two tectonic plates crash together; the rocks crumple upward into gigantic folds.

igneous rock Rock formed when magma becomes solid, especially after it has poured out of a volcano.

lava Hot, liquid rock that comes out of a volcano onto Earth's surface.

magma Hot, liquid rock found below Earth's surface.

mantle The part of Earth below the crust and surrounding the core.

metamorphic rock Rock formed by the action of heat or pressure.

sedimentary rock Rock formed from the sand, stones, mud, etc., that settle at the bottom of lakes.

shock wave A movement of very high air pressure that is caused by an earthquake.

sphere Any object that is completely round, for example, a ball.

tectonic plate One of the huge sheets of rock that form Earth's surface.

Crust to Core

... in 30 seconds

Earth is not perfectly round. It is a squashed sphere that is flatter at the top and bottom. Earth bulges out around the middle, at the equator. The solid, rocky ground you walk on is Earth's crust.

The crust varies in thickness. Under the continents, it is an average of 21 miles (35 km) thick, but it is only 4–6 miles (6–10 km) thick under the oceans.

Beneath the crust is a layer of rock called the mantle. Just under the crust, the mantle is so hot that some of it has melted to make soft, molten rock, called magma.

Under the mantle is Earth's core. It has two layers: the outer core and inner core. The outer core is liquid metal, mostly iron and nickel. The inner core is solid metal, with a superhot temperature of up to 8,100°F (4,500°C). But it does not melt because it is pressed hard by the weight of the layers all around it.

3-second sum-up

Earth is made of different layers, from the crust to the core.

The Center of Earth

The distance from the crust to the center of Earth is about 4,000 miles (6,400 km). If it was possible, it would take you 53 days to walk there without stopping. So far, the deepest hole ever drilled by humans has only reached about 7 miles (12 km) down.

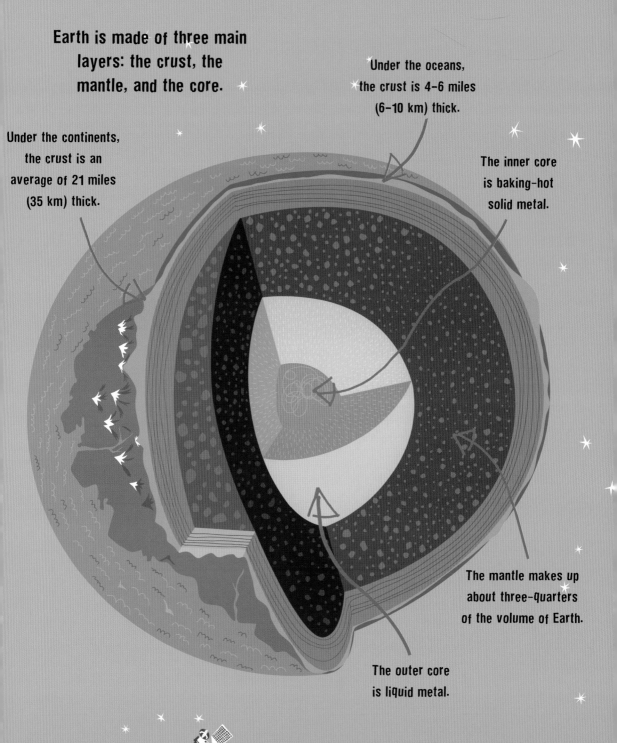

Earth is made of three main layers: the crust, the mantle, and the core.

Under the oceans, the crust is 4-6 miles (6-10 km) thick.

Under the continents, the crust is an average of 21 miles (35 km) thick.

The inner core is baking-hot solid metal.

The mantle makes up about three-quarters of the volume of Earth.

The outer core is liquid metal.

Drifting Continents

... in 30 seconds

The continents are moving! The crust surrounding Earth is cracked into giant pieces, called tectonic plates. There are seven large plates and many smaller ones. The plates move about an inch or so every year, carrying the continents with them. This movement is known as continental drift. The plates drift on the layer of molten magma, beneath, in Earth's mantle.

In some places, the edges of the plates move apart. In other places, they slide past each other. Sometimes, the edges of two plates collide. These movements cause earthquakes and volcanoes, and they build mountains.

Continental drift has been happening for millions of years. About 250 million years ago, all of today's continents were joined together in one supercontinent, called Pangaea. Pangaea later separated into Laurasia and Gondwanaland. Gondwanaland then split to form Antarctica, South America, Africa, India, and parts of Southeast Asia and Australia. Laurasia divided to make North America, Europe, and Asia.

3-second sum-up

Earth's crust is cracked into pieces, which drift slowly.

3-minute mission Oatmeal Plate Tectonics

Ask an adult to help you cook some oatmeal. When it's just been cooked, it is hot and liquid, like the magma of Earth. Let the oatmeal cool a little—the surface will form a cool skin, like Earth's crust. If you reheat it, the surface will move, and bubbles will appear through the "crust," like volcanoes erupting.

Earth's continents drift on seven tectonic plates. Over millions of years, the continents have moved to where they are today.

250,000,000 years ago

There was just one supercontinent, called Pangaea.

Pangaea broke into Laurasia and Gondwanaland.

200,000,000 years ago

Gondwanaland split into Africa and South America. Laurasia then split into North America, Europe, and Asia.

65,000,000 years ago

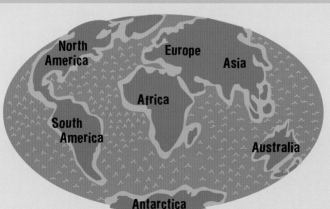

Today

Today, there are seven continents.

Rocks and Minerals

... in 30 seconds

If you dig down into the ground, you will come to solid rock. Rocks are the building blocks of Earth's crust.

Rocks come in all kinds of shapes, textures, and colors. There are three types.

Igneous rocks start as red-hot magma deep inside Earth. The magma rises toward the surface, where it may erupt from a volcano. It cools and hardens to form igneous rocks, such as basalt, granite, and obsidian.

Sedimentary rocks are made from little fragments of rock, sand, and mud that have been eroded and the remains of tiny sea animals. Over millions of years, they are compressed (squashed tightly together) into layers of rock, such as sandstone, limestone, and chalk.

Metamorphic rocks are igneous or sedimentary rocks that are changed by heat deep underground, or by the huge forces that push up mountains. They include marble, slate, and quartzite.

3-second sum-up

Earth's crust is made up of different rocks and minerals.

3-minute mission How Rocks Are Made

Pressure and heat act to make rocks—see how this works.

You need: • 3 slices each of white and whole-wheat bread • Wax paper • Heavy books • Microwave • Adult helper

1 Stack the bread, alternating white and whole-wheat slices. Wrap in wax paper.

2 Place books on the stack to squash it. Then remove the books.

3 Place the bread in the microwave for 1 minute. The heat and pressure make the bread hard—just how rocks are formed.

There are three types of rocks. They form in different ways.

When magma cools, it forms igneous rock.

Magma can reach Earth's surface through a volcano.

Magma comes from the mantle.

Sedimentary rocks are formed from fragments of rock, sand, mud, and tiny sea animals.

Underground, sedimentary rocks are heated and put under pressure because of the weight of the sediment on top of them.

If the rocks are heated to an extremely high temperature, they may form new metamorphic rocks.

Volcanoes

... in 30 seconds

Volcanoes happen when magma and gases from deep inside Earth are put under pressure and force their way to the surface through cracks in the crust. The magma may erupt as streams of red-hot rock or explode in clouds of ash and dust.

There are about 1,500 active volcanoes around the world. Most are located at the edges of Earth's plates.

When magma reaches Earth's surface, it is called lava. It can reach temperatures of more than 2,000°F (1,200°C) and flow at speeds of up to 60 miles (100 km) per hour.

Think of a volcano and you probably imagine a cone-shaped mountain, but not all volcanoes are like that. Their shape depends on how thick the lava is and how violently they erupt. Thick, sticky lava builds tall cones with steep sides. Thin, runny lava builds gently sloping, dome-shaped volcanoes.

3-second sum-up

Volcanoes erupt when magma forces its way to the surface.

Volcanologists

Volcanologists study volcanoes as a job. It's an exciting, challenging, and sometimes dangerous career. Some volcanologists study active volcanoes to try to work out how to protect the people nearby. They may find themselves close to a volcano when it erupts. They'll sense the ground-shaking eruption, hear the loud noises of explosions and breaking rocks, and may even feel some ash pouring down on them. To become a volcanologist, you need to study the sciences, math, and computing.

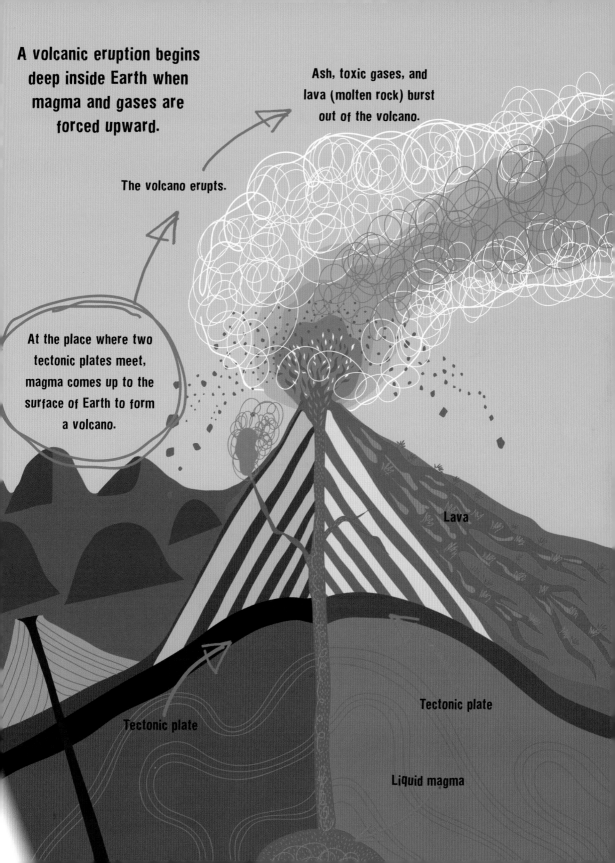

A volcanic eruption begins deep inside Earth when magma and gases are forced upward.

Ash, toxic gases, and lava (molten rock) burst out of the volcano.

The volcano erupts.

At the place where two tectonic plates meet, magma comes up to the surface of Earth to form a volcano.

Lava

Tectonic plate

Tectonic plate

Liquid magma

Earthquakes

... in 30 seconds

Sometimes, the edges of tectonic plates get stuck, but the plates keep moving. They push against each other. Pressure builds up under the ground. Suddenly, the pressure is released. The rocks slip, sending out gigantic shock waves.

The ground shakes violently. It's an earthquake. The shock waves from a massive earthquake can travel thousands of miles around Earth. Buildings can collapse, cars crash, power lines fall, and people may be killed or injured.

Seismologists (earthquake experts) mostly use the Richter scale to measure earthquakes. It grades earthquakes from 0–10, according to their magnitude—the amount of energy released when the rocks break. Each step up the scale means a 30-fold increase in energy. A magnitude 4 quake on the Richter scale is a whopping 900 times more powerful than a level 2 earthquake.

3-second sum-up

An earthquake happens when Earth's plates move suddenly.

3-minute mission Shock Waves

To see how shock waves work, simply throw a pebble in a pond. Watch the waves ripple outward. They are largest where they form, and gradually get smaller as they move away.

If you search on the Internet, you should be able to find some fun animations that show how earthquakes happen.

Earthquakes can be devasting. The sudden movement of the plates causes huge shock waves.

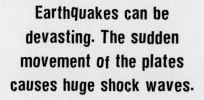

This cross section shows the plates moving—but the edges are stuck.

The rocks suddenly slip. The earthquake waves begin here, at the focus.

The earthquake waves reach the surface at the epicenter, directly above the focus.

The earthquake waves shake the ground.

Mountains

... in 30 seconds

Movements of Earth's crust have created most of the world's great mountains. When two plates crash together, the rocks crumple upwards into gigantic folds—and make fold mountains. The Himalaya mountains in Asia formed like this 40 million years ago.

When faults or cracks in Earth's crust force enormous blocks of rock upward, block mountains form. They have flatter tops than fold mountains. The Sierra Nevada range in North America is formed of block mountains.

Magma under the ground can push upward to build dome mountains. The magma pushes the rocks above into a round bulge. It cools to form solid rock. The Black Hills in North America formed in this way. Volcanoes can erupt and create mountains, too. Mount Kilimanjaro in Tanzania and Mount Etna in Italy formed like this.

Did you know that mountain ranges can stretch for thousands of miles? The longest mountain range on Earth is the Andes in South America. It's about 4,500 miles (7,250 km) long.

3-second sum-up

Earth's crust can shift to create massive mountains.

3-minute mission Mountain Making

Make your own fold mountains.

You need: • 4 strips of modeling clay in different colors • 2 wooden blocks

1 Arrange the strips, one on top of the other, like layers of rock.

2 Put a wooden block at each end to be the plates.

3 Push the blocks toward each other, as if the plates are colliding.

4 The harder you push, the more crumpled the layers will be.

The Himalaya mountains were formed by movements of Earth's crust.

The tectonic plate carrying India crashed into the plate carrying the rest of Asia.

The Himalaya mountains started to form.

Asian plate

Indian plate

The two plates pushed against each other, and Earth's crust was squeezed upward.

They became the highest mountains on Earth—and they are still growing.

Weather and Climate

What is the weather like where you are? The weather happens in Earth's atmosphere, as the sun's rays warm the air. It happens every day, all of the time. Climate is the pattern of weather in a place over a long period of time, from cold and icy at the poles to hot and steamy in the tropics. In this chapter, you'll find out how the rain that drops on you has fallen many times before, and learn about some of the wildest winds on the planet.

Weather and Climate
Glossary

air current The movement of air in a particular direction.

air pressure The force of the air in the atmosphere pressing down on Earth's surface.

alto cloud Middle-level cloud.

atmosphere The mixture of gases that surrounds Earth.

charge (electrical) The amount of electricity that is carried by a substance.

cirrus cloud A type of light cloud that forms high in the sky.

climate The regular pattern of weather conditions of a particular place.

condense To change from a gas into a liquid—for example, when water vapor turns into water.

cumulus cloud A type of thick white cloud that forms low in the sky.

cumulonimbus cloud A high mass of thick cloud with a flat bottom, often seen during thunderstorms.

debris During a tornado, pieces of wood, metal, brick, or trash that are carried away by the strong winds.

evaporate When a liquid evaporates, it changes into a gas—for example, water turns into steam.

exosphere The region near the outer edge of a planet's atmosphere.

eye (of storm) A calm area at the center of a storm.

mesosphere The part of Earth's atmosphere that is between 31 and 53 miles (50 and 85 km) from the ground, between the stratosphere and the thermosphere.

microclimate The weather in a particular small area, especially when this is different from the weather in the surrounding area.

polar Connected with, or near the North Pole or South Pole.

storm surge An unusual rise in the level of the ocean near the coast, caused by wind from a severe storm.

stratosphere The layer of Earth's atmosphere between about 10 and 31 miles (16 and 50 km) above the surface of Earth.

stratus cloud A type of cloud that forms low in the sky, making a gray layer covering the sky.

supercell An extremely powerful thunderstorm.

temperate Having temperatures that are mild, so never particularly hot or cold.

thermosphere The region of the atmosphere above the mesosphere, between about 53 and 300 miles (85 and 500 km) above Earth.

tropical Relating to the tropics, the area just above and below the equator. The climate is warm or hot, and moist all year round.

troposphere The lowest layer of Earth's atmosphere, between the surface of Earth and about 5 to 10 miles (8 to 16 km) above the surface.

vortex A mass of air in a tornado that spins around very fast and pulls things into its center.

water vapor A mass of especially small drops of water in the air.

Earth's Atmosphere
... in 30 seconds

So what's between us on Earth and black space beyond? Our Earth is surrounded by a giant blanket of gases, called the atmosphere. The atmosphere has different layers. We live in the troposphere. It reaches up to 5–10 miles (8–16 km) above Earth's surface. The troposphere provides us with oxygen to breathe.

The air in the troposphere never stays still. It is constantly being moved about by changes in air pressure and temperature. The moving air helps to spread the sun's heat around the world and causes our weather.

Feeling under pressure? The weight of the air in the atmosphere presses down on everything on Earth, including you. This is air pressure. It varies all the time. "Lows" are areas of low pressure, with the lowest pressure in the center. "Highs" are areas of high pressure, with the highest pressure in the center. Lows usually bring wet, cloudy weather. Highs usually bring sunny, dry weather.

3-second sum-up

The atmosphere is a blanket of gases around Earth.

3-minute mission Air-pressure Trick

You need: • Thin cardboard, 3 x 5 inches (7.5 x 12.5 cm) • A glass • Water

1 Fill the glass one-third full with water.

2 Wet the lip of the glass and cover the top with the cardboard. Hold the cardboard in place.

3 Take the glass to the sink and turn it upside down. Carefully, take your hand away.

4 What happens? The force of air pressure against the cardboard should hold the card in place.

The atmosphere is a blanket of gases that surrounds Earth. It is made up of five layers.

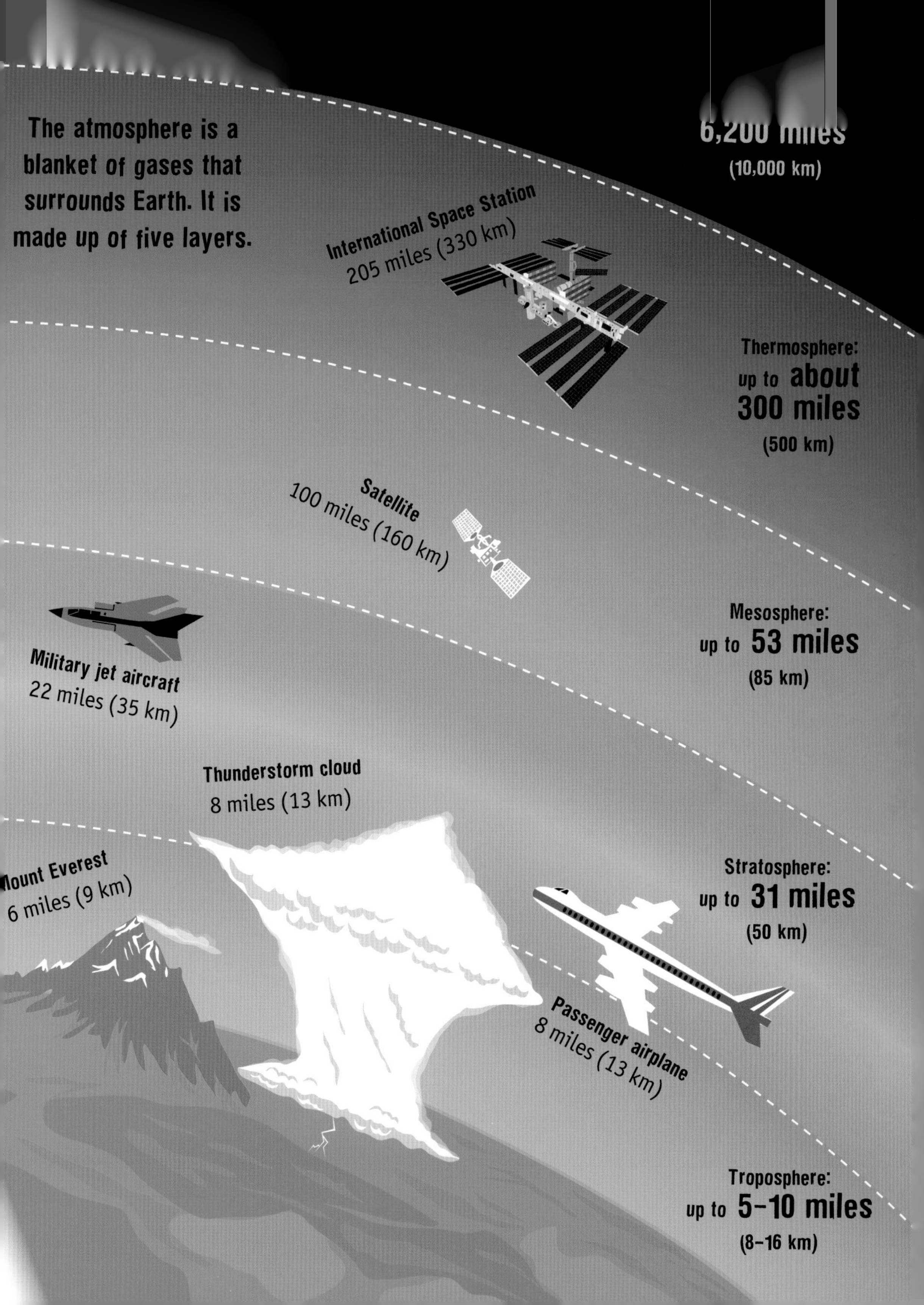

6,200 miles
(10,000 km)

International Space Station
205 miles (330 km)

Thermosphere:
up to about 300 miles
(500 km)

Satellite
100 miles (160 km)

Mesosphere:
up to 53 miles
(85 km)

Military jet aircraft
22 miles (35 km)

Thunderstorm cloud
8 miles (13 km)

Mount Everest
6 miles (9 km)

Stratosphere:
up to 31 miles
(50 km)

Passenger airplane
8 miles (13 km)

Troposphere:
up to 5-10 miles
(8-16 km)

Water Cycle

... in 30 seconds

The water that soaks you when it rains is on a long journey. The sea is where the journey begins. Water evaporates from the sea to form water vapor in the atmosphere. You can't see water vapor, but when the air contains a lot, it feels warm and sticky.

If the water vapor cools, it condenses into tiny droplets of water, or tiny ice crystals. These droplets and crystals make up the clouds you see in the sky. If they grow large enough, they fall from the clouds as rain or snow. Rain and melted snow flow from the land into streams and rivers, which carry the water back to the sea.

Water is constantly moving between the seas, the atmosphere, the land, and rivers and lakes. This circulation of water is called the water cycle.

Clouds are part of the water cycle. Next time you're outside, try to find these types: cumulus (piled, lumpy clouds); stratus (layered clouds); cumulonimbus (rain clouds); and alto (middle-level clouds).

3-second sum-up

The water cycle is the circulation of water on Earth and in the atmosphere.

3-minute mission Making Rain

You need: • Large glass bowl • Warm water • Aluminum foil or plastic wrap • Ice cubes

1 Pour warm water into the bowl until the water is about 2 inches (5 cm) deep.

2 Cut a piece of foil and use it to tightly cover the bowl.

3 Put some ice cubes on top of the foil.

4 Water will evaporate from the bottom of the bowl to form water vapor. When the water vapor hits the cold foil, it will condense and "rain" will drip back into your "sea."

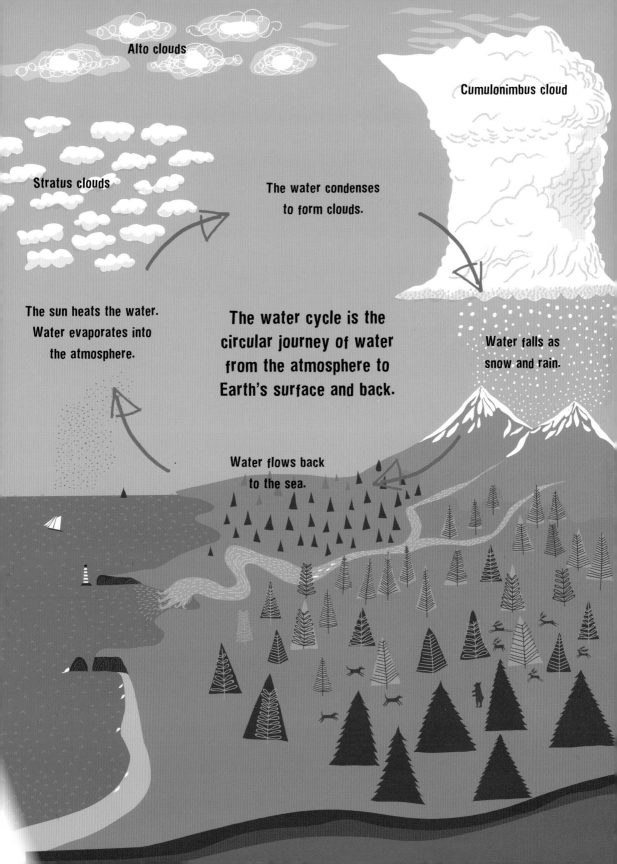

Alto clouds

Cumulonimbus cloud

Stratus clouds

The water condenses
to form clouds.

The sun heats the water.
Water evaporates into
the atmosphere.

The water cycle is the
circular journey of water
from the atmosphere to
Earth's surface and back.

Water falls as
snow and rain.

Water flows back
to the sea.

Thunder and Lightning

... in 30 seconds

As you read this, about 2,000 thunderstorms are raging around the world. Crashes of thunder and flashes of lightning are two of Earth's most spectacular weather events.

Lightning is a superpowerful spark of electricity that jumps through the air. A bolt of lightning heats the air to thousands of degrees Fahrenheit. This heat makes the air expand suddenly, which causes the rumbling boom of thunder.

Thunderstorms happen when cumulus clouds keep growing into towering storm clouds, called cumulonimbus clouds. These can be more than 6 miles (10 km) high. Powerful air currents flow up and down inside the clouds, building up huge electric charges. Positive charges grow in the top of the cloud and negative charges grow in the bottom.

When the charges grow large enough, electricity leaps from one part of a cloud to another, between clouds, or between a cloud and the ground. You see this as lightning. Sheet lightning is a bright flash inside a cloud; forked lightning is a bright streak.

3-second sum-up

Lightning is a spark of electricity that leaps through the air.

3-minute mission Thunderstorm Distance

Light travels much faster than sound, so you see lightning before you hear thunder. It's easy to work out how far away a thunderstorm is.

1 When you see lightning, start counting seconds on a stopwatch.

2 Stop counting when you hear the thunder.

3 Divide the number of seconds by five to work out the distance to the storm in miles (divide by three for kilometers). Sound travels 1 mile every 5 seconds (1 km every 3 seconds). For example, if you count 10 seconds, the distance is 2 miles away.

Hurricanes

... in 30 seconds

Hurricanes are enormous spinning storms. They bring superstrong winds, torrential rain, and towering waves at sea, and they can cause flooding on land.

A hurricane starts as a group of thunderstorms that form over warm, tropical seas near the equator. Sometimes, the thunderstorms develop into a swirling storm, called a tropical storm. Some tropical storms die away, but some carry on growing, drawing energy from the warm sea they pass over. Their winds get stronger and stronger, and they grow into bands of towering clouds full of rain.

When the winds inside a tropical storm reach 74 miles (119 km) per hour, the storm is officially a hurricane. The Saffir-Simpson scale measures the strength of a hurricane, from category 1 to category 5. Category 5 hurricanes bring winds of more than 155 miles (249 km) per hour!

As a hurricane moves across the sea, it pushes up a bulge of water called a storm surge. If the hurricane reaches land, the water can sweep inland, causing flooding. In 2005, the storm surge of Hurricane Katrina severely flooded New Orleans. A hurricane's high winds and heavy rain also cause serious damage.

3-second sum-up

A hurricane is a huge swirling storm with strong winds.

Naming Hurricanes

All hurricanes are given names. The World Meteorological Organization makes up name lists, one for each year. The lists are reused every six years. If a hurricane causes a lot of damage, its name is never used again. Andrew, Mitch, and Katrina are examples of retired names.

Hurricanes form over warm, tropical seas and cause terrible damage and flooding if they reach land.

The wall of cloud around the eye is called the eye wall.

The eye is a cloud-free hole in the center.

Hurricanes spin counterclockwise in the northern hemisphere. In the southern hemisphere, they spin clockwise.

A hurricane brings strong winds, heavy rain, and thunderstorms.

Tornadoes

... in 30 seconds

Did you know that the strongest winds on Earth are found inside tornadoes? Tornadoes are twisting, whirling columns of air that bring winds of up to 300 miles (480 km) per hour. These are strong enough to smash buildings to pieces, toss cars around, and even pluck trains from their tracks.

Tornadoes are formed by extremely energetic thunderstorms, called supercells. Powerful air currents inside a supercell create a spinning column of air, called a vortex, at the bottom of the cell. A tornado happens when this column of air descends from the cell and touches the ground.

The air on the outside of a tornado spirals upward, carrying debris with it. The fast-flying debris can be carried many miles before being dropped back to Earth, causing terrible damage. Tornadoes can measure more than 2 miles (3 km) across, and they move across the ground at speeds of up to 70 miles (115 km) per hour.

3-second sum-up

A tornado is a spinning column of air with extremely powerful winds.

3-minute mission Tornado in a Bottle

You need: • Large, clear glass jar with a lid • Dish-washing liquid • Food coloring • Water

1 Fill the jar with water almost to the top.

2 Add a few drops of food coloring to the water, and a few drops of dish-washing liquid.

3 Swirl the jar around and around to make the water spin around inside it, then stop.

4 Can you see the tornado-like shape inside the jar?

A tornado happens when the air currents inside a supercell thunderstorm form a vortex that touches the ground.

Vortex

Winds blow around the vortex.

The tornado moves across the ground.

Debris is picked up by the winds.

Climate Zones

... in 30 seconds

What kinds of weather do you see in one year? Climate is the pattern of weather that happens in a place over a long period of time. It's not the same as the weather you have from day to day. If you live somewhere that has warm summers, you might get a few cold days in summer, but generally, the weather is warm.

Different parts of the world have different climates. These areas are called climate zones. There are three main climate zones—polar, tropical, and temperate.

Places around the South Pole and the North Pole have a polar climate. It is cold all the time, with freezing-cold winters and no warm summers. Places near the equator have a tropical climate. It is baking hot all year round, and there are dry and rainy times. Places between the equator and the poles have a temperate climate. There are four seasons, with a warm spring and summer, and a cool fall and winter.

Other climate zones exist, too, such as mountain climates, which are cold, wet, and windy, and desert climates, which are very dry.

3-second sum-up

Climate is the pattern of weather over a long time.

Microclimates

Weather experts say that some places have their own microclimate, or local climate. In cities, the heat coming from buildings makes the climate hotter than in the surrounding countryside. It's cold and windy on mountains, but valleys often have a warmer microclimate because they are sheltered from winds.

Polar zone

Polar zone

Temperate zone

Tropical zone

Temperate zone

Polar zone

Temperate zone

Tropical zone

Earth has three main climate zones: polar, tropical, and temperate.

Watery World

A large part of our planet is covered in water. This water lies in the five oceans, and in rivers and lakes around the world. Some is frozen in glaciers and ice sheets. In this chapter, you can discover more about our watery world, from the largest and deepest lakes, to the long journey of rivers from their source to the sea, and the amazing landscape that lies under the oceans.

Watery World
Glossary

arch At the coast, when a cave erodes to form an arch of rock.

bacteria The simplest and smallest forms of life. They exist in large numbers in air, water, and soil, in both living and dead creatures and plants. They are often a cause of disease.

bay A part of the sea, partly surrounded by a wide curve of the land along the coast.

cirque A round, bowl-shape hollow area that forms in the side of a mountain.

crater lake A lake that forms in the crater of a volcano that is not active.

current The movement of water in the sea or a river.

delta An area of land made from sediment laid down by rivers, shaped like a triangle, and where a river may split into several smaller rivers before entering the sea.

erode To gradually destroy and remove the surface of something through the action of wind, rain, or other natural elements.

estuary The wide part of a river where it flows into the sea.

evaporate When a liquid evaporates, it changes into a gas—for example, water turns into steam.

floodplain An area of flat land beside a river that becomes flooded when there is too much water for the river to hold.

glacier A large mass of ice, formed by snow on mountains, that moves, usually very slowly, down a valley.

gravity The force that attracts objects in space toward each other, and that pulls objects on Earth toward the center of the planet, so that things fall to the ground when they are dropped.

headland An area of high land that sticks out from the coast into the sea.

magma Especially hot liquid rock found below Earth's crust.

meander A curve in a river.

mineral A substance naturally present in Earth and not formed from animal or vegetable matter—for example, gold and salt.

moraine A mass of soil and rock carried along by a glacier and left when it melts.

mouth (river) The place where a river joins the sea.

oxbow lake A lake that forms when a bend in a river becomes cut off from the river.

rift lake When the movement of Earth's tectonic plates makes huge blocks of rock rise or fall, a rift lake can form in the hollow.

seamount A mountain under the sea.

sediment Sand, stones, mud, and other materials carried by water or wind and left—for example, on the bottom of a lake or river.

snout (glacier) The end of a glacier, where the ice melts.

stack At the coast, when an arch of rock collapses to leave just a column of rock.

tectonic plate One of the huge sheets of rock that form Earth's surface.

tide The regular rise and fall in the level of the sea, caused by the pull of the moon and sun.

trench A deep valley in the ocean floor.

Oceans and Seas

... in 30 seconds

Do you know why Earth is known as the Blue Planet?
It's because more than two-thirds of its surface is covered by water.
There are five oceans: the Pacific, Atlantic, Indian, Southern, and Arctic.

The Pacific Ocean is the largest. It stretches nearly halfway around
the globe. It's almost as big as all of the other oceans put together.
The Arctic is the smallest. For most of the year, the Arctic Ocean is
covered in ice.

A sea is a smaller area of water that forms part of an
ocean. For example, the Mediterranean Sea is in the
Atlantic Ocean, and the Arabian Sea is in the Indian
Ocean. Many seas are at least partly enclosed by land.

About 97 percent of all Earth's water lies in the oceans. This
water is salty because of the minerals (mostly common salt)
that have dissolved in it. Most of the salt comes from rocks
on land that are washed into the sea by the rain and rivers.
Some comes from volcanoes under the sea.

3-second sum-up

Oceans and
seas cover
more than
two-thirds
of Earth.

Ocean Currents

The water in the oceans is constantly moving. The wind drives
along currents—huge bands of water that flow through the sea
like rivers. Some currents carry warm water; others, cold water.

Currents help to spread heat around the world, and they have
an important effect on the weather of the places they flow past.

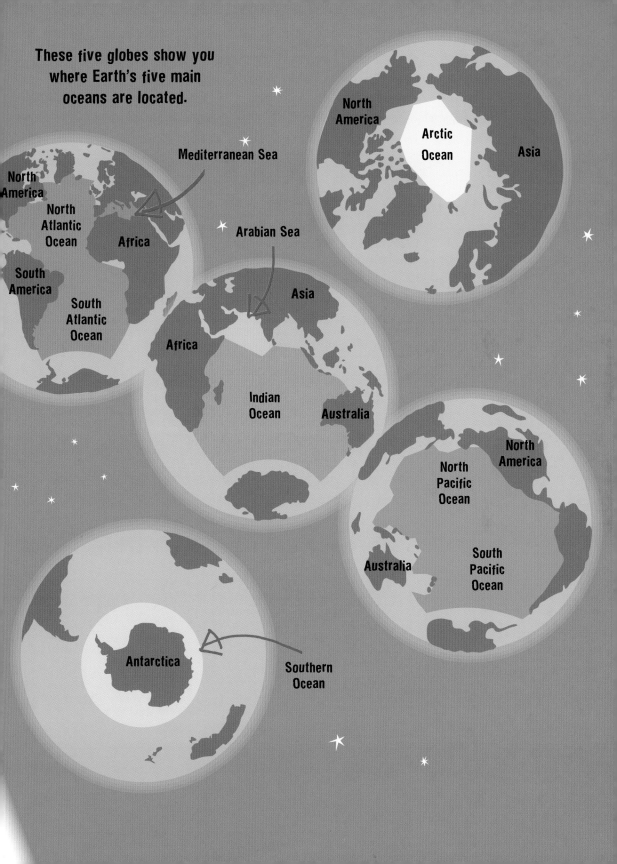

These five globes show you where Earth's five main oceans are located.

Under the Sea

... in 30 seconds

The top layers of the sea are brightly lit by the sun, but as you dive farther down, it quickly gets darker. Below a depth of about 330 feet (100 m), it is pitch black and extremely cold.

A remarkable landscape lies beneath the sea. On the ocean floor, there are vast, flat plains, covered with sediment made from the remains of sea plants and animals. Long chains of mountains, called ocean ridges, form where tectonic plates move apart, allowing magma to rise up.

There are also single mountains, called seamounts, some of which are higher than the highest mountains on land. Trenches are deep valleys in the ocean floor.

Deepest of all is the Mariana Trench in the Pacific. The bottom of this trench is 36,070 feet (10,994 m) below the ocean surface. If Mount Everest, the highest mountain in the world, was placed in the Mariana Trench, it would be covered by 1 mile (1.6 km) of water.

3-second sum-up

Beneath the sea are flat plains, high mountains, and deep trenches.

Black Smokers

Along some ocean ridges, superhot, dark-colored water shoots out of vents (openings) in the seabed. These vents are known as black smokers. Minerals in the water form chimneylike structures around the vents. Groups of animals live around black smokers. The animals include giant 6-foot (2-m)-long tube worms, crabs, and shrimp. They live on bacteria that grow by using the minerals in the vent water.

At the edge of a continent, the seabed slopes downward to the ocean floor.

An amazing landscape lies beneath the sea, from high mountains to deep trenches.

The continental shelf is an area of shallower sea along the edges of a continent.

The ocean floor is between about 11,500 and 14,750 feet (3,500 and 4,500 m) below the surface.

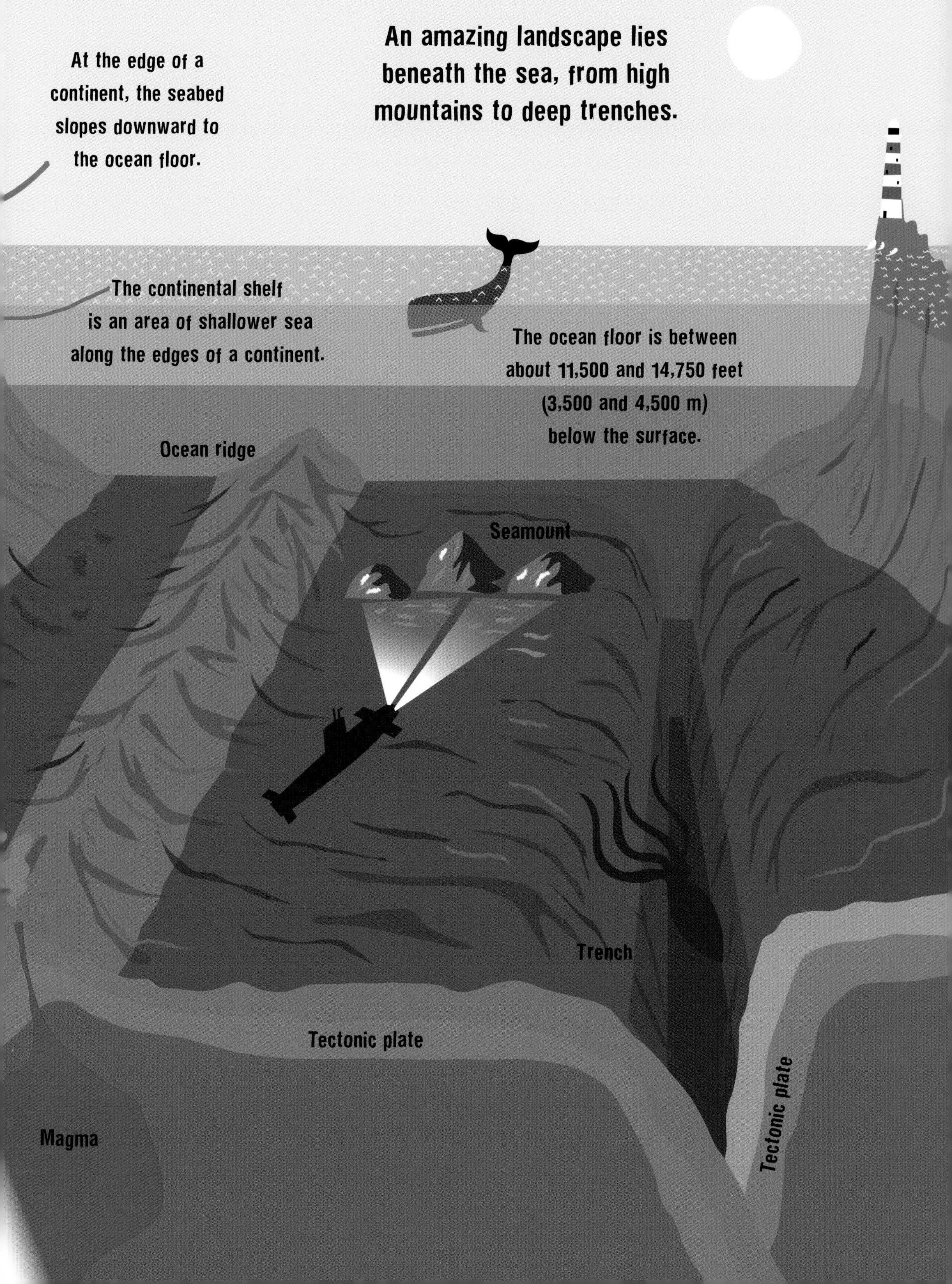

Ocean ridge

Seamount

Trench

Tectonic plate

Tectonic plate

Magma

Coasts

... in 30 seconds

At the coast, the sea meets the land. Here, the powerful forces of the wind and waves erode the rocks. They reshape the landscape, carving out cliffs, caves, and arches.

Estuaries are places where rivers meet the sea. The coast bends inland at an estuary. Estuaries have low-lying mud banks that are uncovered at low tide.

In most areas, the sea rises and falls on the shore twice a day with the tides. It's the pull of the moon's gravity on Earth that causes tides.

Gravity pulls on the water in the oceans, making the water build up on the side facing the moon. The water also builds up on the opposite side. These places have high tide. As Earth spins, places move in and out of the areas pulled by the moon, so they have low tide and then high tide again.

The sun also plays a part in the tides. It makes them higher and lower at different times of year.

3-second sum-up

Coasts are where the sea meets the land.

3-minute mission Bending Waves

You need: • Large, deep baking pan • Cup
• Rectangular plastic lid

1 Pour ½ inch (1 cm) of water into the baking pan.

2 Stand the cup upside down in the middle of the pan.

3 Make small waves in the water with the edge of the lid.

4 The waves will bend around the cup to meet on the other side. This is how waves bend around headlands on coasts.

Rivers
... in 30 seconds

Just one percent of the water on Earth flows in rivers and fills lakes. This is fresh water. Rivers carry water from the land to the sea. On the way, they shape the landscape that they flow through.

As it flows, a river carries along a load of sediments (rock, mud, and clay). The rocks wear out the riverbed, carving out valleys. Some of this load—mostly the mud and clay—is dumped on the river's floodplain, where it creates rich land ideal for farming.

Near the sea, the river reaches its final stage. At its mouth, it flows into the sea. Here, it dumps more sediment, which builds up a fan-shape area of new land, called a delta.

The Nile is Earth's longest river. It flows for 4,160 miles (6,695 km) through many different countries in Africa, and it has made one of the world's largest deltas.

3-second sum-up

A river carries water from the land to the sea.

3-minute mission Make River Sediment

You need: • Large baking pan • Piece of wood an inch or so thick • Play sand • Pitcher of water • An outdoor space (this is messy)

1 Cover the baking pan with a layer of sand about ¼ inch (6 mm) thick. Raise one end of the pan on the wood.

2 Slowly pour some water onto the raised end of the pan. Watch what happens to the sand.

3 The water carries the sand down the pan and drops it at the other end—just as a river carries sediment.

A river flows through the
landscape, shaping it
along the way, and
carrying water to the sea.

Upper stage: A river begins at
its source, high up in the hills
or mountains. It flows fast
down the steep slopes.

In its middle stage, the
river flows more slowly.
It swings from side to side
in huge meanders.

On each side of the river
is a floodplain, which is
covered with water when
the river floods.

At its mouth, the river
flows into the sea. It may
dump more sediment to
form a delta.

Lakes

... in 30 seconds

Make a hollow in the ground and pour in a lot of water. You have made a mini lake. That's all a lake is—a hollow filled with water.

There are different kinds of lakes. In mountainous areas, many lakes form in hollows gouged out by ancient glaciers. Oxbow lakes form in river meanders that have been cut off from the river.

When the movement of Earth's tectonic plates makes huge blocks of rock rise or fall, rift and fault lakes form in the hollows. Crater lakes form in the craters of nonactive volcanoes.

How does water reach lakes? Fresh water comes from streams and rivers flowing into them, melted ice from glaciers, or water seeping up from underground. Rainwater falls on them, too.

Some lakes are salty. They form where water dissolves salty minerals from the lake-bed rocks. As the water evaporates, it leaves the salts behind. Large saltwater lakes, such as the Caspian Sea, are called inland seas.

3-second sum-up

A lake is a hollow in the landscape filled with water.

The Largest and Deepest Lakes

The largest lake on Earth is Lake Superior, one of North America's Great Lakes. It covers 31,700 square miles (82,100 sq km), about the area of 66 million Olympic swimming pools. The deepest lake is Lake Baikal in Russia. Its maximum depth is 5,387 feet (1,642 m)—that's just over a mile deep.

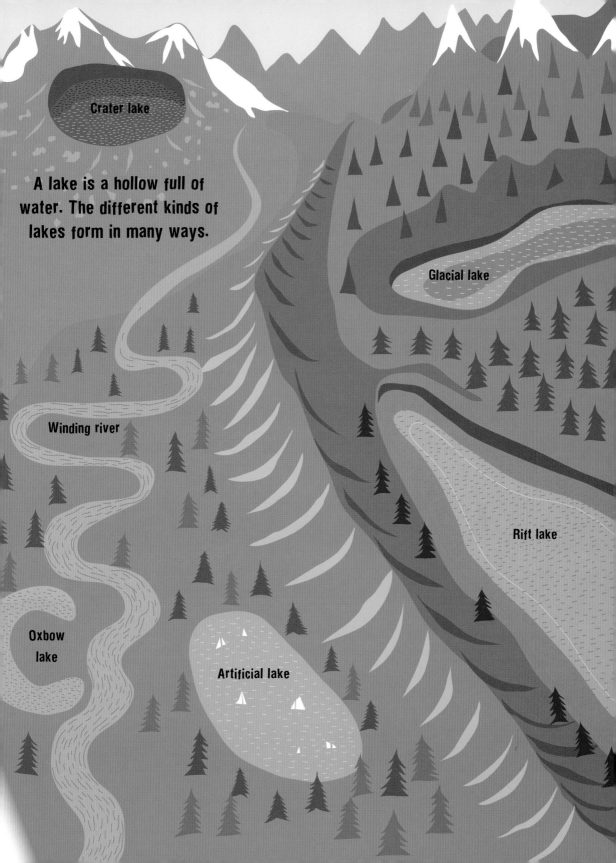

Crater lake

A lake is a hollow full of water. The different kinds of lakes form in many ways.

Glacial lake

Winding river

Rift lake

Oxbow lake

Artificial lake

Glaciers

... in 30 seconds

If you climb to the peaks of the world's highest mountains, you'll see nothing but snow all year round. Gradually, over thousands of years, the deep layers of snow on the mountaintops turn to ice.

They form a great icy river called a glacier, which slides slowly downhill. It's hard to see a glacier moving. A typical glacier moves along at about 6 feet (2 m) a day.

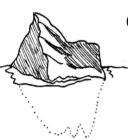

Glaciers also flow from the ice caps—the enormous, thick sheets of ice that cover Antarctica and Greenland.

Over time, glaciers carve out hollows in mountain slopes, called cirques, and U-shape valleys with steep sides and flat bottoms.

The end of a glacier is called its snout. Here, the ice melts as it arrives, dumping pieces of rock that it has carried along.

Many glaciers end in oceans or lakes. Huge chunks of ice break off and crash noisily into the water.

3-second sum-up

A glacier is a slow-moving river of ice.

3-minute mission Glaciers From Space

You need: • Computer (or tablet or smartphone) with the Google Earth application

1 Open Google Earth.

2 Key in "Himalaya mountains" in the "search" box.

3 Zoom in to see the Himalaya mountains in more detail.

4 Key in "Mount Everest." Can you see the glaciers that flow from its slopes?

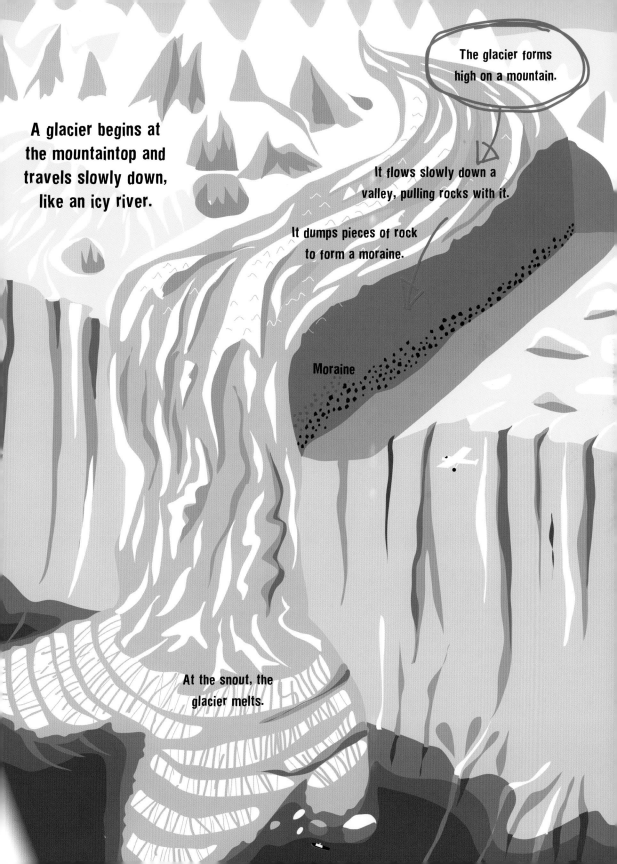

Amazing Ecosystems

An ecosystem is a community of living things (plants and animals) along with nonliving things (rocks, air, and water) that work together and depend on each other to survive. An ecosystem can be as big as a desert or as small as a puddle. In this chapter, you can read about some of Earth's great ecosystems, from steamy rainforests to isolated islands, freezing-cold poles, and colorful coral reefs.

Amazing Ecosystems Glossary

axis An imaginary line through the center of Earth, around which it turns.

canopy The second to top layer of the rainforest, where the tree tops spread over the forest like a roof.

continent One of the large land masses of Earth, such as North America, Europe, Asia, or Africa.

coral reef Structures in the sea made from rock created by tiny animals found in the water.

ecosystem All the living and nonliving things found in a particular area.

emergent layer The top layer of a rainforest, where very tall trees grow above the canopy.

equator An imaginary line around Earth at an equal distance from the North and South poles.

isolation Being in isolation means being separate from everything else.

lowland rainforest A kind of rainforest found around the equator that has a lot of rainfall. Lowland rainforests are found on low land, up to 3,170 feet (1 km) above sea level.

mammal Any animal that gives birth to live babies and feeds its young on milk. Horses, humans, and whales are all mammals.

mangrove rainforest Rainforest that grows in coastal areas in the tropics—the trees can cope with salty water from the sea.

montane rainforest Rainforest that is found in mountain areas.

oasis An area in the desert where there is water and where plants can grow.

poles The two points, known as the North Pole and South Pole, at the opposite ends of Earth's axis.

polyp (coral) A small and very simple sea creature with a body shaped like a tube.

rainforest A thick forest in tropical parts of the world that have a lot of rain.

rain shadow An area that has little rainfall because hills shelter it from the winds that bring rain.

sand dune A hill of sand formed by the wind, near the sea or in a desert.

tropics The area just above and below the equator. The climate is warm or hot, and moist all year round.

understory In a rainforest, the second layer up from the forest floor—little sunshine reaches this area.

Deserts

... in 30 seconds

Picture a desert and you probably imagine vast areas of scorching hot sand. But not all deserts are sandy. Some are rocky or stony. Antarctica is icy. In sandy deserts, the wind blows the loose sand into gigantic piles, called sand dunes, which can be hundreds of yards high.

All deserts are dry. Some are far inland, where rain rarely falls. Some form along the edges of mountain ranges. Any rain will fall on the mountains, not the land alongside.

The Atacama Desert lies in the rain shadow of the Andes Mountains. Parts of it have had no rain for hundreds of years.

Many deserts, such as the Sahara in Africa, are baking hot in the daytime all year round. Some, such as the Gobi in northern Asia, are very cold in the winter. All deserts are cold at night.

Some amazing plants and animals live in these harsh conditions. They have special survival features. Camels can go for days without drinking and weeks without eating. They turn the fat in their humps into food and save water by producing dry droppings.

3-second sum-up

A desert is a place where it hardly ever rains.

3-minute mission Blow a Dune

You need: • An old baking pan • Play sand

1 Do this experiment outdoors. Put a handful of sand on the baking pan and shape it into a model sand dune.

2 With your mouth at the same level as the edge of the pan, blow gently across the dune.

3 Can you see the sand blowing up one side of the dune and down the other?

In a sandy desert, dunes are
shaped by the wind. Some plants
and animals have adapted to live
in the harsh conditions.

Star dune—
a star-shaped dune

Barchan dune—
a crescent-
shaped dune

Acacia tree

Seif dune—a long,
narrow dune

Camels

Transverse dune—
a long dune lying at
right angles to the
wind direction

An oasis is an area of water in
a desert, which usually comes
from water underground.

Monitor
lizard

Sand viper

Rainforests

... in 30 seconds

Rainforests grow in the tropics, on either side of the equator. The climate is hot and humid, and rain pours down almost every day. More than two-thirds of the world's plant species are found in tropical rainforests.

Rainforests cover about 6 percent of Earth's surface. They include lowland rainforests, such as the Amazon; montane rainforests, which grow on mountain slopes; and mangrove forests, which grow along coasts.

The largest is the Amazon rainforest, along the banks of the Amazon River in South America. It's twice the size of India.

There may be hundreds of species of plants and animals living in an area of rainforest about the size of a football field. The most common animals are insects, but hundreds of birds, primates, reptiles, spiders, and frogs live there, too.

3-second sum-up

Rainforests are hot and have a lot of rain.

Rainforest Plants

Rainforest plants contain many useful substances and foods:

- Latex, the sap of the rubber tree, and the raw material for making rubber. The rubber is used to make tires.

- Foods, such as Brazil nuts, cashew nuts, coffee, mangoes, and bananas.

- Bamboo and rattan, used for making furniture.

- The ingredients for some of our favorite treats—cocoa for making chocolate and vanilla for ice cream.

Tropical rainforests are home to hundreds of different species of plants and animals.

Emergent layer

Toucan

Scarlet macaws

Blue macaw

Howler monkey

Canopy

Spider monkey

Sloth

Tamarin monkey

Squirrel monkey

Boa constrictor

Understory

Tapir

Forest floor

Jaguar

Poles

... in 30 seconds

Go to the very ends of Earth and you'll find the poles. They are at either end of Earth's axis—an imaginary line running through Earth from north to south.

At the North and South poles, it is icy and bitterly cold. The North Pole lies in the middle of the Arctic Ocean, which is frozen all year round. The area of ice grows in winter and shrinks in summer. The South Pole is in Antarctica, a huge continent covered with a thick sheet of ice.

The poles are cold all year round, but they get extremely cold in winter. In Antarctica, temperatures can fall as low as -76°F (-60°C). The sun never rises in the middle of winter, but never sets in the middle of the short summer.

Animals, such as polar bears, penguins, and seals, have adapted to life in the freezing polar conditions. They fend off the cold with thick layers of fur, feathers, or fat.

3-second sum-up

At the North and South poles, it is cold all the time.

3-minute mission Floating Iceberg

You need: • Drinking glass • Ice cube • Ruler

1 Fill the glass halfway with water. Drop in an ice cube to make a model iceberg.

2 Very slowly add water until the glass is full to the brim.

3 Using your ruler, estimate how many inches—or millimeters—of your iceberg is above the surface and how much is below.

4 You should find that there is about nine times as much under the water as above.

The Arctic has polar bears, reindeer, foxes, and other mammals.

The Arctic has plants and trees.

North Pole

Arctic

Only a few plants and animals can survive at the North and South poles.

Antarctic   South Pole

The Antarctic has no plants or trees.

The Antarctic has penguins and sea mammals, but no land mammals, except human explorers.

Islands

... in 30 seconds

An island is a piece of land surrounded on all sides by sea. Islands range from tiny coral islands just a few yards wide to enormous continental islands hundreds of miles across. Some islands are low-lying; others have high mountains.

Islands have a wide variety of climates, from hot and wet in the tropics, to cold and wet toward the poles. They are often windy places, with no shelter from winds blowing across the sea.

Greenland is the world's biggest island. Three-quarters of the island is covered in a thick ice sheet. It is warmer around the coast, and this is where most people live.

Many islands are home to plants and animals that are not found in any other part of the world. Because of the islands' isolation, their wildlife has evolved differently. The Galapagos Islands lie off the west coast of South America. They are home to giant tortoises 5 feet (1.5 m) long. They have evolved with long necks for feeding on tall plants.

3-second sum-up

An island is a piece of land surrounded by water.

3-minute mission Floating Seeds

If seeds float to an island, they may grow into plants there.

You need: • Large bowl • Seeds or fruit, such as dried beans and peas, apple, Brazil nuts, sunflower seeds

Think about whether each seed or fruit will float or sink. Test each one. Let the seeds float in water for as long as possible to see if they might reach land without sinking.

Plants and animals travel to islands from other places. They settle and breed, eventually evolving into unique species.

The wind carries seeds.

Birds and bats eat fruit, and the seeds come out in their poop.

Sea turtles, and some other animals, can swim to islands.

Lizards, and animals that can't swim well, may travel on a floating branch.

Coconuts float.

Coral Reefs

... in 30 seconds

Brightly colored fish dart through clear, sparkling water among coral shaped like trees, fans, and even brains. Welcome to the coral reef.

Reefs are home to a huge variety of animals, including two-thirds of all ocean fish, sponges, starfish, and crabs.

Coral is living material, made up of thousands of tiny animals, called polyps. The polyps have soft bodies protected by hard, chalky cases that they build around themselves. When a polyp dies, its body rots away, but its hard case is left behind.

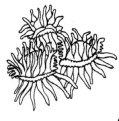

New polyps grow on top of the old cases, and, over many years, the cases build up into different shapes, with living coral on the outside. Over hundreds and thousands of years, groups of coral join together to form long reefs.

Coral mostly grows in warm, shallow water. This is why coral reefs are mostly found in the tropics—along coasts and around the tops of underwater mountains.

The Great Barrier Reef in Australia is the world's largest coral reef. It covers about 86 million acres (35 million hectares)—about the size of 70 million football fields!

3-second sum-up

Coral reefs are built by living animals.

3-minute mission The Great Barrier Reef

You need: • Computer (or tablet or smartphone) with the Google Earth application

1 Start up Google Earth.

2 Find Australia and navigate to the northeast coast.

3 Can you see the Great Barrier Reef along the coast?

It takes 1,000 years for coral polyps to build a new reef!

Coral reefs are built up by tiny animals called polyps, creating a unique habitat for all kinds of sea life.

Polyp larva

Jellyfish

Bottlenose dolphin

Blue shark

Starfish

Stingray

Clown fish

Sea fan

Sea horse

Angelfish

Coral crab

Sea sponges

Octopus

Future Earth

What will Planet Earth be like in the future? Nobody knows, of course. One thing does seem certain—it is changing at a fast rate. All over the world, the weather is getting wilder and precious ecosystems are being destroyed. Many of these changes are due to human activities, but it's not all bad news. In this chapter, you can find out more about what is happening and about what can be done to help to save Earth.

Future Earth
Glossary

atmosphere The mixture of gases that surrounds Earth.

carbon dioxide A gas breathed out by people and animals and also produced by burning carbon.

climate The regular pattern of weather conditions of a place.

coral reef Structures in the sea made from rock created by tiny animals found in the water.

drought A long period of time when there is little or no rain.

ecosystem All the living and nonliving things found in a particular area.

erode To gradually destroy and remove the surface of something through the action of wind, rain, or other natural elements.

extinct When a plant or animal no longer exists because it has died out.

global warming The problem of the rise in temperature of Earth's atmosphere, which is caused by the increase of particular gases, especially carbon dioxide, including those produced by human activity.

greenhouse effect The gradual rise in the temperature of Earth's atmosphere, caused by naturally occurring gases, such as carbon dioxide, which trap the heat of the sun.

landfill An area of land where waste material is buried under Earth's surface.

pollute To add dirty or harmful substances to land, air, or water so that it is no longer pleasant or safe to use.

rainforest A thick forest in tropical parts of the world that has a lot of rain.

recycle To turn things that have already been used into something that can be used again.

resource A supply of something that a country or people can use.

solar power Turning energy from the sun's rays into energy that people can use.

species A group of animals or plants that are similar and able to breed with each other.

thermostat A device that measures and controls the temperature of a machine or room by turning the heating or cooling system on and off as needed.

wind power Turning the energy of the wind into useful energy that people can use.

Changing Climate

... in 30 seconds

Did you know that the climate changes over time?
Scientists believe that today's climate may be changing faster than at any time in the last 10,000 years.

The climate can change naturally. However, most experts agree that today's changes are happening faster because of human activities.

To understand how, we need to head off into the atmosphere. Some of the gases in Earth's atmosphere trap heat from the sun. This is called the greenhouse effect, and it keeps our planet warm. The gas that traps most heat is carbon dioxide.

Every day, human activities, such as burning coal, oil, and gas, give off carbon dioxide. The carbon dioxide rises into the atmosphere. It traps heat, making Earth warmer. Scientists call this global warming. The changing climate is making the weather wilder. We're seeing more storms, floods, and droughts.

We can help reduce global warming by using less fuel for energy and transport and by developing fuels that produce less carbon dioxide. Trees absorb carbon dioxide, so cutting down fewer trees and planting new trees are ways to help our planet.

3-second sum-up

Climate change is a change in weather patterns.

Cutting Energy Costs

It is easy to cut down energy costs at home. Your thermostat should be set to the lowest comfortable temperature—between 64 and 70°F (18 and 21°C). If a family turns down the thermostat by just one degree, it can save $100 (£65) a year. And the household will have saved about 575 pounds (260 kg) of the greenhouse-gas carbon dioxide from going into the atmosphere.

Greenhouse gases trap the sun's heat, causing global warming.

Some heat escapes into space.

The sun's rays warm Earth.

Carbon dioxide and other gases are trapped in the atmosphere.

These gases make it harder for heat to escape.

Carbon dioxide levels are increased by burning fuels and forests.

Power station

We can help reduce global warming by planting trees and using wind and solar power.

Wind farm

Solar farm

Planting trees

Fighting Waste

... in 30 seconds

Every year, we use about 500 billion plastic bags. That's about 70 for each person—and most of them are thrown away. We also throw away a huge amount of plastic bottles, metal cans, and paper.

Most waste is burned or buried in the ground. This buried garbage is called landfill. Some of it will take thousands of years to rot away, and we're quickly running out of suitable places for landfill sites.

But much of our waste can be reused or recycled, so that we use fewer resources and create less garbage. We can often reuse plastic bottles before recycling them.

If we recycle our cans, it saves energy. Making aluminum cans from old ones uses up only one-twentieth of the energy needed to make new ones. A plastic bag made from recycled polyethylene uses one-eighth of the amount of water needed to make a new one. We can also help to fight waste by buying recycled products.

3-minute mission Make a Plant Container

You need: • Clean 2-liter plastic soda bottle • Handful of gravel • Potting mix • A few plant seeds • Scissors • An adult helper

1 Ask an adult to cut around the bottle about one-third up from the bottom.

2 Put a 1-inch (2-cm) layer of gravel in the bottle bottom. Cover with 2 inches (5 cm) of potting mix.

3 Push in the seeds and water them.

4 Make four vertical 1-inch (2-cm) cuts to create flaps in the top rim of the bottle bottom. Slot the top of the bottle into the flaps.

5 Put the plant container on a sunny windowsill and water regularly.

Watch the seeds grow.

3-second sum-up

Our waste pollutes the environment.

Waste materials, such as paper, glass, plastic, and cans, can all be recycled to make new products.

Toy

Shoes

T-shirt

Gift wrapping paper

Juice drink carton

Puzzle pieces

Earrings

Bottles

Material for road surfacing

Marbles

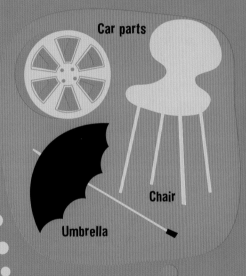

Car parts

Chair

Umbrella

Paper

Glass

Plastic

Cans

Vanishing Habitats

... in 30 seconds

All over the world, humans are destroying wildlife habitats, putting plants and animals in danger. People clear habitats to make space for new homes, factories, and farmland. These pollute the water in our rivers and along our coasts.

When a habitat is destroyed, plants and animals have to adapt to the new conditions or find somewhere else to live. If they cannot, they may die out.

Rainforest habitats are at great risk. Every second, the world loses a patch of rainforest about the size of a football field. People chop down trees for wood and to clear space for mines and farms. Hundreds of species of rainforest plants and animals are wiped out, and the lives of rainforest people are destroyed, too.

Pollution, mining, and the collecting of rare corals and shells threaten coral reefs. About 25 percent of reefs have already been destroyed, and another 60 percent are at serious risk.

3-second sum-up

Many habitats around the world are being destroyed.

3-minute mission Extinct or Under Threat?

Many species of plants and animals have already become extinct, and many more are on the brink of dying out. Look up the animals listed. Are they extinct, or under threat? What is their habitat and what is happening to it?

Species:
Orangutan
Sumatran rhino
Sun bear
Black spider monkey
Tree kangaroo

Saving Earth

... in 30 seconds

Here are some ideas for things YOU can do to help to save Earth.

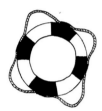

- Join an eco-club at school or gather some friends to start one up. Decide on your campaign. Can you persuade people to cut energy or water use around the school?

- Talk to your friends and family about saving fuel by walking, bicycling, or taking the bus for some journeys instead of traveling by car.

- Remember to turn off the lights when you leave the room and spend a minute less in the shower. You'll save money as well as precious energy.

- Reuse as many items at home as possible. Plastic bottles, cardboard, and scrap paper are handy for all kinds of craft activities. Make sure the materials no one can use any more go in the recycling box.

- Join with some friends to raise some money for an eco-project, for example, saving a threatened habitat.

3-second sum-up

You can help to save the planet in many ways.

The Three Rs

Remember to focus on the three Rs—that's Reduce, Reuse, and Recycle.

Reduce: See if you can walk more often instead of traveling by car.

Reuse: Take your old clothes and toys to a thrift shop.

Recycle: Make sure glass bottles, paper, and cans are recycled.

Discover More

FICTION BOOKS

Attack of the Shidas: AKAs Save Planet Earth! by Muthoni Muchemi, Kindle Edition **(Storymoja and Worldreader, 2012)**

Stories For a Fragile Planet by Kenneth Steven **(Lion Children's Books, 2012)**

NONFICTION BOOKS

Discover Science: Planet Earth by Barbara Taylor and Deborah Chancellor **(Kingfisher, 2011)**

Encyclopedia of Planet Earth by Anna Claybourne and Gill Doherty **(Usborne Publishing Ltd., 2013)**

Explorers: Planet Earth by Daniel Gilpin and Peter Bull **(Kingfisher Books Ltd., 2014)**

Horrible Geography of the World by Anita Ganeri **(Scholastic, 2010)**

How the World Works: A Hands-On Guide to Our Amazing Planet by Christiane Dorion **(Candlewick Press, 2010)**

Planet Earth by Katie Daynes **(Usborne Publishing Ltd., 2008)**

Planet Earth! A Kids Book About Planet Earth by Alexander G. Michaels **(Kindle Edition, 2013)**

Planet Earth—The World in Infographics by Jon Richards and Ed Simkins **(Wayland, 2013)**

Story of Planet Earth by Abigail Wheatley **(Usborne Publishing Ltd., 2013)**

Why Does Earth Spin?: And Other Questions about Our Planet by Mary Kay Carson **(Sterling, 2014)**

DVDs—suitable for all ages

Frozen Planet—The Complete Series by David Attenborough
(2entertain, 2011)

Inside Planet Earth (Demand DVD, 2013)

Planet Earth: The Complete Series by David Attenborough
(2entertain, 2010)

WEB SITES

An Ecological System
http://www.geography4kids.com/files/land_ecosystem.html
All about ecosystems

The Earth's structure
*http://www.bbc.co.uk/schools/gcsebitesize/science/ocr_gateway_
pre_2011/rocks_metals/3_does_the_earth_move1.shtml*
Earth's structure, plate tectonics, rocks

Information and Facts about Rivers
http://primaryhomeworkhelp.co.uk/rivers.html
Features of rivers, flooding, pollution

National Geographic—Climate and Weather
*http://www.watchknowlearn.org/Video.aspx?VideoID=3929&Categor
yID=2671*
Video about the differences between climate and weather

Planets for Kids
http://www.planetsforkids.org/planet-earth.html
The planets in our solar system

What is happening in the ocean?
http://climatekids.nasa.gov/ocean/
About oceans and climate

Weather and climate
http://climatekids.nasa.gov/menu/weather-and-climate/
Pages on all aspects of climate change

Index

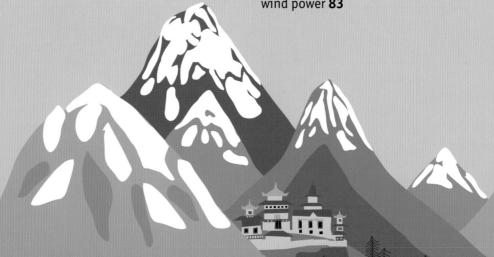